"There is a use for almost everything."

— GEORGE WASHINGTON CARVER

GEORGE WASHINGTON CARVER

BY CHARLES W. CAREY JR.

GRAPHIC DESIGN
Robert E. Bonaker / Graphic Design & Consulting Co.

PROJECT COORDINATOR
James R. Rothaus / James R. Rothaus & Associates

EDITORIAL DIRECTION
Elizabeth Sirimarco

COVER PHOTO
Portrait of George Washington Carver / Corbis-Bettman

Library of Congress Cataloging-in-Publication Data
Carey, Charles W.
George Washington Carver / by Charles W. Carey, Jr.
p. cm.
Summary: A biography of the man who was born a slave in
Missouri and who overcame many hardships before going
on to become a college professor known for his
accomplishments in the field of agriculture.
ISBN 1-56766-569-1 (library reinforced : alk. paper)

1. Carver, George Washington, 1864?-1943 — Juvenile literature.
2. Afro-American agriculturists — United States —
Biography — Juvenile literature. 3. Agriculturists — United
States — Biography — Juvenile literature.
[1. Carver, George Washington, 1864?-1943. 2. Agriculturists.
3. Afro-Americans — Biography.] I. Title

S417.C3C27 1999   98-47048
630'.92 — dc21   CIP
[B]   AC

Contents

A Young Boy in Missouri   6

School Days   13

A New Career   17

A Life of Invention   25

Timeline   37

Glossary   38

Index   39

A Young Boy in Missouri

In the early 1860s, George Washington Carver was born on a farm near Diamond, a small town in southwestern Missouri. At the time, many states and territories in the United States, including Missouri, permitted *slavery*. George's mother Mary was a slave on the farm of a man named Moses Carver. Carver was a kind person who treated her more like a member of the family than a slave.

At birth, children born to slaves became the property of their parents' master, so George and his older brother Jim were slaves as well. George's father was probably a slave on a nearby farm who died not long after he was born.

When George was still an infant, bandits from nearby Arkansas kidnapped him and his mother. Moses offered to give the bandits a $300 racehorse in exchange for the return of Mary and her baby. The bandits took the horse but kept Mary. George and Jim never saw their mother again. The bandits probably returned George to Moses only because he suffered from *whooping cough,* and they thought he might not survive.

In 1865, at the end of the American Civil War, the United States abolished slavery. George and Jim were free, but they were alone in the world. The young brothers had no parents to protect them and no money to support themselves. Moses Carver and his wife Susan decided to let the brothers move into their farmhouse.

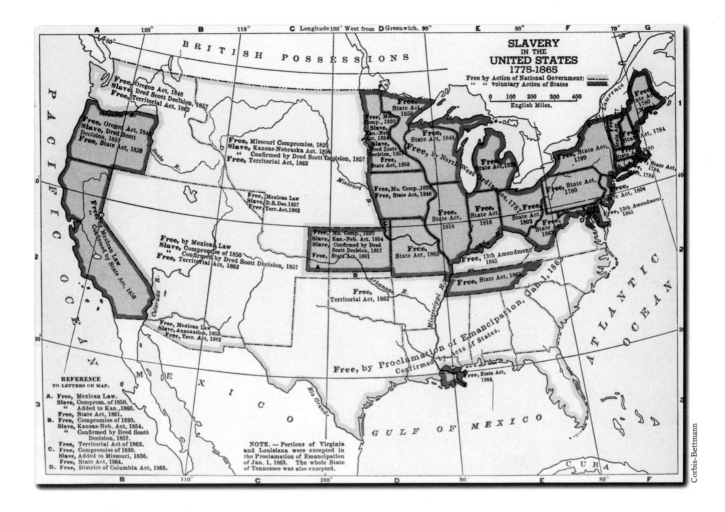

SLAVERY
IN THE
UNITED STATES
1775-1865

Corbis-Bettmann

ALTHOUGH HE WAS BORN A SLAVE IN THE SLAVE STATE OF MISSOURI, THE AMERICAN CIVIL WAR ENDED WHILE GEORGE WAS STILL VERY YOUNG. WHEN THE WAR WAS OVER, THE U.S. GOVERNMENT FREED AFRICAN AMERICAN SLAVES.

Tuskegee University Archives

MOSES CARVER WAS FIRST GEORGE'S OWNER AND
LATER HIS FOSTER FATHER. MOSES WAS KNOWN
TO HAVE A SPECIAL TALENT WITH ANIMALS. A PET
ROOSTER WAS OFTEN SEEN PERCHED ON HIS
SHOULDER, AND HE COULD FEED WILD SQUIRRELS
FROM HIS HAND. MOSES HELPED TO INSPIRE
GEORGE'S LOVE OF NATURE.

George and Jim were almost like sons to the Carvers. George, who continued to have health problems, was too frail to help Moses and Jim with the farm chores, so Susan taught him other tasks. He helped with all the household chores, including the family's cooking, cleaning, sewing, and laundry. She also taught him how to read from an old spelling book. Moses taught George to play the violin. George was an intelligent boy. Whatever he wanted to learn, he quickly mastered.

George also spent much of his time wandering in the woods that surrounded the Carver farm. He loved nature and passed hours inspecting the insects and reptiles he found. Sometimes he would bring the creatures home and hide them. Susan found out, so she began to ask George to empty his pockets before entering the house. His favorite playthings were all the different plants that grew in the area. He collected the seeds of the prettiest wild flowers and planted them in a secret garden. George seemed to have a natural talent for nursing sick plants back to health. Even as a young boy, he was known around the small town of Diamond as "the plant doctor."

Tuskegee University Archives

GEORGE SPENT THE FIRST **30** YEARS OF HIS LIFE STRIVING FOR AN EDUCATION. HE HAD LITTLE EXPERIENCE WITH PREJUDICE UNTIL HE TRIED TO ATTEND THE PUBLIC SCHOOL IN HIS HOME TOWN, BUT FINDING A SCHOOL THAT ACCEPTED BLACK STUDENTS WAS AN ONGOING CHALLENGE.

Soon George yearned to learn more than Susan's spelling book could teach him. The Carvers could not instruct him, because they had little education themselves. Diamond's public school, which met at the town's small church, accepted George and Jim at first. Shortly after they began attending classes, however, some of the town's White citizens demanded the school suspend all Black children. The event was George's first real experience with *prejudice*.

In 1876, when George was about 11 years old, the Carvers found a young man to tutor him. After only a few months, bright young George already knew more than the tutor did. George was certain there was much more he could learn. "I wanted to know the name of every stone and flower and insect and bird and beast," he would later recall, "I wanted to know where it got its color, where it got its life — but there was no one to tell me." George set out to investigate the world.

National Park Service, George Washington Carver National Monument

WOODS AND FOREST SURROUNDED THE CARVER FARMHOUSE. IT WAS IN THIS ENVIRONMENT THAT GEORGE LEARNED TO LOVE NATURE.

National Park Service, George Washington Carver National Monument

THIS STATUE OF YOUNG GEORGE IS LOCATED IN DIAMOND, MISSOURI, ON THE LAND WHERE HE GREW UP, NOW THE GEORGE WASHINGTON CARVER NATIONAL MONUMENT.

National Park Service, George Washington Carver National Monument

GEORGE (LEFT) AND HIS BROTHER JIM (RIGHT) BOTH ATTENDED THE PUBLIC SCHOOL IN NEOSHO, BUT WHILE LEARNING TO READ AND WRITE SATISFIED JIM, GEORGE WANTED TO CONTINUE HIS STUDIES.

School Days

When he was about 12 years old, George said good-bye to Moses and Susan and moved to Neosho, Missouri, where he could attend a public school for *African Americans*. In Neosho, George lived with a Black couple named Andrew and Mariah Watkins. In exchange for room and board, he helped Mariah with the housework. After two years, George outgrew the school in Neosho, just as he had outgrown the tutor back in Diamond. It was time to move again, this time to Fort Scott, Kansas.

Over the next five years, George lived in several small Kansas towns, attending the local public school and earning money to support himself by cooking, washing clothes, or doing odd jobs. In one town, there was another young man named George Carver, so George gave himself the middle name Washington so people would not get the two of them confused.

In 1884, at age 19, he graduated from the high school in Minneapolis, Kansas. George wanted to attend college, so he applied to a small school in Highland, Kansas. Impressed by his excellent grades, Highland College accepted him by mail, but when George arrived for the first day of classes, school officials would not allow him to attend. They turned George away because he was Black.

George felt discouraged and almost gave up his dream of attending college. He bought some land in western Kansas where he grew wheat and lived by himself for a few years, earning the repect and friendship of many settlers in the area. Later he traveled across Kansas and Iowa, doing small jobs or opening small laundry businesses wherever he briefly settled.

In 1890, George decided it was time to get over the disappointment of being barred from Highland College. He applied to Simpson College in Iowa, and the school accepted him as a student. When he showed up for classes, George was not turned away.

George took many classes at Simpson College, including grammar, arithmetic, art, essay writing, voice, and piano. He often brought in some of the plants he had grown for his art teacher, Miss Etta Budd, to admire. His knowledge of plants impressed her, and she suggested he transfer to Iowa State College where her father was a professor of horticulture (the study of plants). When he was about 30, George became the first African American to attend Iowa State College.

It was not long before George became one of the best students at Iowa State. He learned to breed two plants from different species to make a *hybrid*, or "child" plant. Scientists create hybrids to be stronger, prettier, or bear better-tasting fruits and vegetables than the "parent" plants.

George received a bachelor of science degree in 1894 but decided to stay at Iowa State a while longer. The horticulture department asked him to teach classes, and George became the school's first African American faculty member. He also managed the school's greenhouse and studied for an advanced degree in plant science. In 1896, George received a master's degree in *agriculture*.

GEORGE LOVED TO PAINT, BUT HE KNEW IT MIGHT BE DIFFICULT TO SUPPORT HIMSELF AS AN ARTIST. HE DECIDED TO TAKE THE ADVICE OF HIS ART TEACHER AND STUDY HORTICULTURE AT IOWA STATE COLLEGE.

Tuskegee University Archives

AFTER HE COMPLETED HIS STUDIES AT IOWA STATE
COLLEGE, GEORGE ACCEPTED A TEACHING POSITION
AT THE TUSKEGEE INSTITUTE IN ALABAMA.

A New Career

After graduation, George received offers to teach botany at several colleges. One offer was from Booker T. Washington, head of the Tuskegee Institute in Alabama. Tuskegee was a college for African Americans that Washington founded in 1881. The school taught primarily *vocational skills* that would help young Black men and women find jobs after graduation.

The Civil War had ended less than 20 years earlier. Blacks were no longer slaves, but they now had a difficult time finding good jobs — particularly in the South, where they were often victims of *racism*. Whites did not want to work side-by-side with African Americans, nor did they want them to take jobs that Whites could have. Blacks struggled to find a satisfactory means to support themselves.

Many Blacks in the South earned their living by farming. Washington wanted George to teach Tuskegee students everything he knew about agriculture. He could not offer a large salary, but George decided to go to Tuskegee. Like Washington, George wanted to help Blacks improve their lives.

George may have had another reason for accepting Washington's offer. He had always been the only African American at every school he attended. Although he made friends with his teachers and fellow students, the laws of *segregation* usually prevented him from socializing with Whites outside the classroom. This would not be a problem at Tuskegee, where all the teachers and students were African Americans.

In 1896, George became the head of Tuskegee's agriculture department. He had moved around a great deal in his early life to attain his goals, but after he arrived at Tuskegee, he never moved again.

Tuskegee did not have enough money to hire all the employees it needed, so all the teachers had to pitch in and do extra jobs in addition to their teaching duties. George directed an experiment station where the workers tried to grow hybrids. At the same time, he managed the school's two regular farms where dairy cows, chickens, honeybees, fruit trees, and vegetables were raised. Because there was no veterinarian, he had to take care of the sick animals.

Washington also charged George with keeping the school grounds neat and green, as well as purchasing school supplies at the most affordable price. He was even asked to make sure that all drivers obeyed the speed limit on school grounds. On top of all this, he had to make time to attend numerous meetings with other faculty members.

CARVER ARRIVED AT TUSKEGEE INSTITUTE IN 1896. IN THE YEARS THAT FOLLOWED, HE REALIZED THAT THE SCHOOL WAS VERY DIFFERENT FROM IOWA STATE COLLEGE. HE HAD MANY RESPONSIBILITIES, LEAVING LESS TIME TO SPEND IN THE CLASSROOM AND LABORATORY.

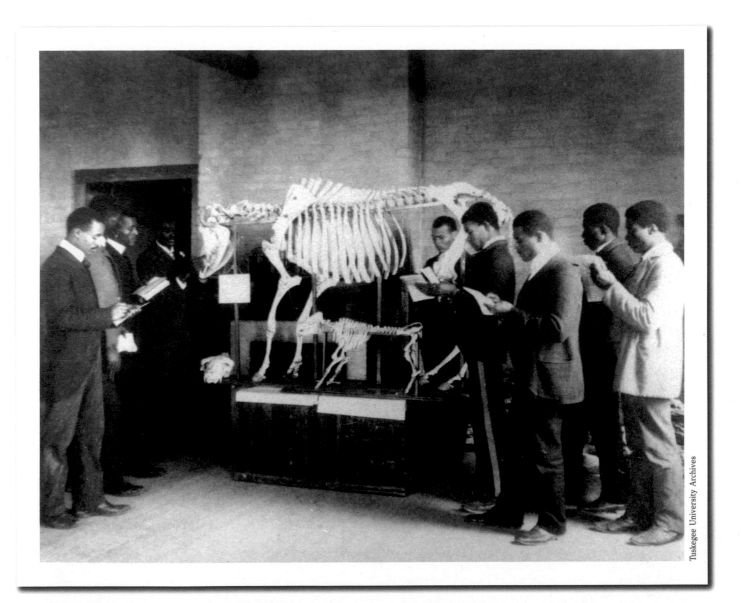

AT TUSKEGEE GEORGE TRIED TO SHOW HIS STUDENTS
THAT ALL FORMS OF SCIENCE — FROM BOTANY TO
BIOLOGY — WERE RELATED TO ONE ANOTHER.

Corbis-Bettmann

STUDENTS PARTICIPATED IN A WIDE VARIETY OF EXPERIMENTS
IN CARVER'S LAB AT THE TUSKEGEE INSTITUTE.

George did not want to do all these extra jobs. He did not like to tell people what to do, and he felt that attending meetings was often a waste of time. Perhaps his biggest problem at Tuskegee was that the school did not give him enough money to buy supplies and hire staff to get his jobs done. Tuskegee simply did not have much money available for such things. When he got to Tuskegee, George discovered that his laboratory was nothing more than an empty room. He was expected to find or make all of the equipment himself.

George had so many different responsibilities that he could not always do his extra jobs as well as he would have liked, which caused disagreements with Washington. From the time George arrived at Tuskegee until Washington died in 1915, the two men had many arguments about George's extra jobs and how much help the school should give him. What George really wanted was to spend his time experimenting with plants and teaching others what he knew. It was at these tasks that he excelled.

Unlike most other colleges, Tuskegee accepted anyone who applied. Since southern states spent little money on public high schools for African Americans, Tuskegee took in many students who were not ready for more difficult college studies. George had to find a new way to communicate with his students, who were different from the White students at Iowa State. He developed a different teaching style from the one he had used before.

Instead of standing in front of the classroom and lecturing to his students in a formal way, George talked with them as if they were having a friendly conversation. He also explained that every subject he taught, including agriculture, botany, and chemistry, was related to the other subjects — and even to other things like farming and cooking. Sometimes he explained things by telling jokes, and other times he related the lesson to a story from the Bible, a book most southern Blacks knew well.

George taught his students by letting them discover things for themselves. He sent them out into the woods that surrounded the institute to search for plants and insects, much as he had done when he was a child. He awarded prizes for the most interesting finds. He encouraged students to conduct their own experiments and gave them helpful suggestions when they made mistakes. Most of all, George inspired his students by teaching them to appreciate the miracles and beauty of nature. George was a popular teacher. Perhaps because he never married and had no children of his own, he treated all of his students as if he were their father.

Although he often teased them, jokingly threatening to spank them if they did not do better in school, he always gave them love and respect. He taught them to treat themselves and others the same way. George was an important influence in the lives of his students, most of whom never forgot him.

Long after they left Tuskegee, many of his former students continued to write letters to him, and he always wrote back as soon as he could. A large number also named their firstborn sons after him. He always remembered these "grandchildren" on their birthdays and graduations.

National Park Service, George Washington Carver National Monument

GEORGE OFTEN TOOK HIS STUDENTS OUT TO THE FIELDS THAT SURROUNDED THE TUSKEGEE INSTITUTE WHERE HE COULD EXPLAIN MANY OF THE CONCEPTS HE TAUGHT IN CLASS.

UPI/Corbis-Bettmann

GEORGE'S ASSISTANT, DR. AUSTIN CURTIS JR., CONDUCTS
AN EXPERIMENT IN A LAB AT THE TUSKEGEE INSTITUTE.

GEORGE LOVED TO TEACH, BUT THE TIME HE SPENT IN
HIS LABORATORY WAS EQUALLY IMPORTANT TO HIM.

A Life of Invention

In addition to teaching, George conducted many laboratory experiments at Tuskegee. His goal was to invent farming methods that would make life easier for poor southern farmers. He also aimed to invent interesting uses for plants that no one had thought of before.

At the time George arrived at Tuskegee, most southern farmers grew almost nothing but cotton. Growers could usually sell it for enough money to buy everything else they needed, from tools for the farm to food to feed their families. George developed an improved species of the cotton plant, which became known as Carver's Hybrid. This new breed of cotton matured quickly, and farmers could pick it before insects such as the boll weevil had a chance to destroy the crops.

Carver's Hybrid did not solve one problem: Southern farmers planted more cotton than the land could support. All plants need to absorb *nutrients* from the soil, just as human beings absorb nutrients from the foods they eat. Cotton crops leech many important nutrients out of the soil, particularly nitrates — important substances that help plants grow. The only way to grow cotton in the same fields year after year is to use *fertilizer* to replenish the nitrates. Most Black farmers had just enough money to rent land, buy farm tools, and feed their families. There was little income left to pay for fertilizer, forcing the farmers to grow less cotton every year until it became difficult for them to make a living at all.

George tried to help these farmers by finding ways to enrich the soil without using expensive fertilizer. He discovered that *legume* plants actually returned nutrients to the soil, acting as natural fertilizer. George began to encourage farmers to practice a method of planting called *crop rotation* in which growers alternate one type of crop with another to enrich the soil. Black-eyed peas were one legume that many southerners enjoyed eating.

George taught farmers to alternate black-eyed pea crops with cotton crops. By doing so, growers could improve the quality of their soil without spending money on commercial fertilizer. It also gave them something inexpensive and nutritious to feed their families, as well as to sell at the market. George also formulated 40 new recipes using black-eyed peas, including pancakes and pudding, to encourage more people to buy them.

Corbis-Bettmann

GEORGE KNEW THAT SOIL LOST NUTRIENTS IF FARMERS GREW ONE TYPE OF CROP IN THE SAME FIELDS YEAR AFTER YEAR. HE BEGAN TO EDUCATE SOUTHERN FARMERS ABOUT THE IMPORTANCE OF ROTATING THEIR CROPS EACH YEAR.

COTTON HAD BEEN THE SOUTH'S MOST IMPORTANT CROP SINCE EUROPEANS FIRST CAME TO AMERICA, BUT IT HAD TAKEN TOO MANY NUTRIENTS FROM THE SOIL. CARVER CONVINCED MANY SOUTHERN FARMERS TO REPLACE THEIR COTTON CROPS WITH LEGUMES.

IN 1941, THE UNIVERSITY OF ROCHESTER IN NEW YORK HONORED CARVER AND HIS RESEARCH. UNIVERSITY OFFICIALS EXPLAINED TO CARVER THAT THEY WERE HONORING HIM "BECAUSE YOU HAVE OPENED DOORS OF OPPORTUNITY TO THOSE AMERICANS WHO HAPPEN TO BE NEGROES; BECAUSE YOU HAVE ONCE AGAIN DEMONSTRATED THAT IN HUMAN ABILITY, THERE IS NO COLOR LINE."

George continued to experiment with other ways to help farmers raise inexpensive food. He invented a way to grow large sweet potato crops on a small piece of land, then he showed farmers how to make *staples* such as flour, sugar, and bread — all from sweet potatoes. George also demonstrated how farmers could afford to eat more meat by feeding their hogs acorns instead of expensive corn meal. Acorns were plentiful in southern forests, and people could harvest them free of cost.

George introduced soybeans and alfalfa to southerners, two plants that they usually did not grow. Farmers could sell both products to factories that made paint and animal feed. Today George is considered the father of *chemurgy*, the science of finding industrial uses for plant products.

George is most famous for introducing the peanut to southern growers. Although peanuts had been grown throughout the South in the past, they were mostly used to feed livestock. George proved that peanuts, like other legumes, could build up the soil while also providing farmers, their families, and the marketplace with an inexpensive source of *protein*. As farmers started growing more peanuts, supplies soon exceeded what livestock could consume, so George set out to find new uses for them.

ONCE GEORGE PROVED HOW VALUABLE PEANUTS COULD BE, MANY SOUTHERN FARMERS BEGAN TO GROW THEM IN THEIR FIELDS.

Corbis-Bettmann

George was not the first to suggest that peanuts could be an important crop. Several experts at the U.S. Department of Agriculture had predicted that people could use peanuts for a variety of things. An Englishman discovered how to make peanut milk two years before George started his peanut experiments. It was George, however, who put these theories — and hundreds of his own inventions — to good use.

Peanuts contain plenty of vegetable oil, which can be used to make many other things. George invented more than 300 uses for peanuts — from cheese to facial powder, shampoo to printer's ink. He taught people to make items such as vinegar, a coffee-like drink, soap, medicine, and wood stain from peanuts.

AP Wide World Photos

THOUSANDS OF YOUNG POLIO VICTIMS WROTE TO THANK GEORGE FOR PROVING THAT PEANUT OIL COULD BE USED IN THE TREATMENT OF THE DISEASE.

Corbis-Bettmann

CARVER'S AMAZING DISCOVERIES EARNED HIM
THE NICKNAME "THE WIZARD OF TUSKEGEE."

UPI/Corbis-Bettmann

IN 1942, AUTO MANUFACTURER HENRY FORD PRESENTED GEORGE WITH A MODERN, FULLY-EQUIPPED LABORATORY IN WHICH TO CONDUCT HIS RESEARCH. GUESTS AT THE CELEBRATION ENJOYED SANDWICHES AND SALADS THAT GEORGE MADE FROM WEEDS AND WILD VEGETABLES.

Perhaps the most popular product George developed was peanut butter. George ground roasted peanuts to make a smooth, creamy butter. It lasted longer than butter made from milk because it did not have to be kept cold. Others had made butter from corn oil, but peanut butter was more nutritious because it contained more protein. After the people in the peanut industry heard about George's latest invention, they did everything they could to promote the new product. Soon people all over the country were spreading peanut butter on bread to make a delicious, nutritious, and inexpensive snack. Thanks to George, children all over the world enjoy peanut butter sandwiches for lunch.

George Washington Carver researched and taught at the Tuskegee Institute for 47 years. He labored not for fame or fortune, but to quench his thirst for knowledge — and to help people. Carver never applied for a *patent* for any of his important discoveries, which would have allowed him to make money from the sale of any products derived from them. "God gave them to me," he once said. "How can I sell them to someone else?"

His contributions helped southerners, both Black and White, overcome the poverty and ignorance that plagued the South during his lifetime. He proved that African Americans could contribute a great deal to their nation if only given the education and opportunities they deserved.

George Washington Carver died on January 5, 1943. He left his life savings to Tuskegee to establish a museum and a research institute for agricultural chemistry on the school's campus. The George Washington Carver Foundation is still in existence today. Carver was buried at the Tuskegee Institute along with its founder, Booker T. Washington. The words on his gravestone read, "He could have added fortune to fame, but caring for neither, he found happiness and honor in being helpful to the world."

Ten years after George's death, the United States government declared his birthplace in Diamond, Missouri, a national monument. The park stretches across 210 acres of what was once Moses Carver's farm. Thousands travel to the monument each year.

A museum at the site includes exhibits about Carver's life and his many important discoveries. Beyond the museum is a short trail that winds through the Missouri woodland and prairie, the very landscape that inspired Carver to become a scientist.

PROFESSOR CARVER'S
First Laboratory

Corbis-Bettmann

GEORGE'S FIRST LABORATORY, CONSISTING OF SIMPLE, HOMEMADE EQUIPMENT, IS ON EXHIBIT AT THE GEORGE WASHINGTON CARVER MUSEUM, LOCATED AT THE TUSKEGEE INSTITUTE.

Library of Congress/Corbis

GEORGE WASHINGTON CARVER DIED ON JANUARY 5, 1943. HE DONATED HIS LIFE'S SAVINGS TO BUILD A RESEARCH LABORATORY AND MUSEUM AT THE TUSKEGEE INSTITUTE.

National Park Service, George Washington Carver National Monument

Timeline

1860   George is born a slave in Diamond, Missouri.

1865   The American Civil War ends, and slaves are freed.

1876   The Carvers hire a tutor to teach George.

1877   George moves to Neosho, Missouri, to attend a school for African Americans.

1879   George moves to Fort Scott, Kansas, to attend another school.

1884   George completes high school in Minneapolis, Kansas.

1885   George is refused entrance to Highland College because he is Black.

1890   George enters Simpson College in Iowa.

1891   George is admitted to Iowa State College (then called Iowa Agricultural College) and becomes the first African American to attend the school.

1894   George receives a bachelor of science degree from Iowa State College.

1896   George receives a master of science degree from Iowa State College. He travels to Alabama where he will teach at the Tuskegee Institute.

1897   George begins his experiments with sweet potatoes.

1902   George begins his experiments with black-eyed peas.

1903   George begins his experiments with peanuts.

1908   George demonstrates how to make 40 different foods from black-eyed peas.

1915   George develops a type of cotton that becomes know as Carver's Hybrid.

1916   George demonstrates 105 different uses for peanuts, including the most popular — peanut butter.

1918   George demonstrates 115 different uses for sweet potatoes.

1943   George dies in Tuskegee, Alabama.

1953   The George Washington Carver National Monument is established.

Glossary

African Americans
Americans whose ancestors came from the African continent.

agriculture
The science of cultivating soil, raising crops, and preparing crops for use.

chemurgy
The science of using raw materials, especially farm products, in industry.

crop rotation
The practice of planting different crops in the same field from year to year to enrich the soil.

fertilizer
A substance that puts nutrients into the soil to make it more fertile, or able to support plant growth.

hybrid
A plant that is grown by mixing the seeds, roots, or other parts of two different plants. The tangelo tree, for example, was created by combining a tangerine tree and a grapefruit tree.

legume
A member of the family of plants whose roots contain a bacteria that replaces or maintains the nitrogen in soil. The fruit of many legumes are important sources of food, such as beans, peanuts, and peas.

nutrients
Chemicals that living things need in order to live, usually taken in by eating or drinking.

patent
An official document, usually granted by a government, that gives an inventor the exclusive right to make, use, or sell his or her invention.

prejudice
A bad feeling or opinion about something or someone without just reason; feeling anger toward a group or its characteristics.

protein
A vital nutrient that is an essential building block of all living cells. People and animals obtain protein by eating plant or meat products.

racism
The belief that one race is naturally superior, or better, than another.

slavery
The practice of forcing another individual or group of individuals to labor without pay.

segregation
The separation or isolation of a race, class, or ethnic group.

staples
Basic food products that are used by people all around the world, such as flour and sugar, for which the demand is constant.

vocational skills
Skills or trades that are taught with the intent that they will help an individual pursue a related career.

whooping cough
A disease that causes severe coughing and sometimes loud, uncomfortable breathing.

Index

African Americans
   and education, 9, 10, 17, 21-22
   and farming, 17, 25
   and jobs, 17
   and racism, 9, 10, 13, 17
American Civil War, the, 6, 7, 17
animal feed, 29

black-eyed pea, 26
Budd, Etta, 14

Carver, George Washington
   and art, 14-15
   birth of, 6
   childhood of, 6-13
   death of, 33-35
   education of, 9-10, 12-15
   and illness, 6, 9
   kidnapping of, 6
   and parents, 6
   and prejudice, 9, 10, 13
   students of, 16, 19, 21-22
   and teaching, 14, 16, 19-22
   and Tuskegee Institute
      donation of life's savings to, 33, 35
      responsibilities at, 18, 21
      years spent at, 33
Carver, Jim, 6, 9-10, 12
Carver, Moses, 6, 8, 9-10
   farm of, 6, 9, 10, 34
Carver, Susan, 6, 9-10
Carver's Hybrid, 25
chemurgy, 29
Civil War, the, *see* American Civil War
cotton, 25-26, 27
crop rotation, 26-27
Curtis, Austin Jr., 23

farming, 17, 25-26, 27, 29-30
fertilizer, 25-26
Ford, Henry, 32

George Washington Carver Foundation, 33
George Washington Carver National Monument, 11, 34

Highland College, 13-14
hybrids, 14, 18, 25

Iowa State College, 14-15, 18, 21

legumes, 26, 27, 29

patent, 33
peanut, 29-30, 33
peanut butter, 33
polio, 30
protein, 29, 33

Rochester, University of, 28

segregation, 17
Simpson College, 14-15
slavery, 6-7, 17
soil, nutrients and, 25-26
staples, 29
sweet potatoes, 29

Tuskegee Institute, the, 16-23, 25, 33, 34, 35
   classes offered at, 17
   founding of, 17
   lack of money at, 17, 18, 21

Washington, Booker T., 17-18, 21, 33
Watkins, Andrew and Marian, 13

For Further Information

Durant, Penny Raife. *Exploring the World of Plants.* Danbury, CT: Franklin Watts, 1995.

Nicholas, Lois P. and William Epes. *George Washington Carver.* Broomall, PA: Chelsea House Publishers, 1994.

Pollack, Steve. *Find Out About Plants.* Bbc Publications, 1996.

Web Sites
African Americans in Science
http://www.lib.lsu.edu/lib/chem/display/faces.html

George Washington Carver Home Page
http://www.norfacad.pvt.k12.va.us/project/carver/George.htm

National Park Service Georege Washington Carver Monument
http://www.coax.net/people/LWF/carver.htm